Pick Up Your Crown

Thank You Kelly

♡ Jessica

Shaday

Jessica Simington

Pick Up Your Crown© 2020
Written By: Jessica Simington

Published By: Pen Legacy®
Layout & Formatting By: U Can Mark My Word
Edited By: Abigail Summer
Cover Design & Layout: Tia-Allyse Watson

Library of Congress Cataloging – in- Publication Data has been applied for.

ISBN: 978-1-7351424-7-0

PRINTED IN THE UNITED STATES OF AMERICA.

This book is dedicated to God. I want to thank my mentors who God placed in my life to keep me focused. You are appreciated.

Table of Contents

INTRODUCTION 7

CROWN OF REJECTION 9

TAINTED CROWN 13

EMOTIONALLY ABUSED CROWN 17

IMMATURE CROWN 21

CROWN OF BITTERNESS 25

CROWN OF ILLUSION 29

BATTERED CROWN 37

CROWN OF INSANITY 43

CROWN OF RAGE 49

SUICIDAL CROWN 53

CROWN OF SELF-AWARENESS 57

CROWN OF RESEMBLANCE 61

CROWN OF DOUBLE MINDEDNESS 67

CROWN OF ACCOUNTABILITY 69

PICK UP YOUR CROWN 73

Introduction

"Sometimes in life, your situation will keep repeating itself until you learn your lesson." ~ Anonymous

No matter how well we map out our lives, sometimes things don't go as expected. This book is about the many unexpected turns I experienced in my life. I used to carry the shame of not meeting important deadlines I set for my life. The dream of obtaining a master's degree by age 24, finding my prince charming and starting a family at age 25, and touring the world as an actress at age 26. Let's not forget purchasing a home by age 27 while living debt free. Now, I can laugh at the unmet expectations, but there was a time I was filled with so much disappointment from not accomplishing certain milestones. This book is to encourage you that your life is still destined for greatness despite what it may look like or your current level. God created us all for a purpose and He knew all the stops and turns you would make beforehand.

To see why I continued to go in a cycle of chaos, I had to sit still before God and find the root to my problem. This book explores my relational patterns that influenced unhealthy decisions that kept me in my valley experience. I want to be clear that although I mentioned situations with certain people, I do not blame them for the choices I made and I hold myself accountable for every decision. To move forward, we must be forgiving, take accountability, and seek God for fulfillment.

This book is not about pointing fingers or what he/she did to me, rather it's a testament that I don't look like what I have been through. There was no magical wand that was waved before my eyes. There was no microwavable fix. It took me time with God, tearful nights, a lot of journaling, prayer, inspirational quotes and motivational speeches. Even though I am still on my journey of success, this is a document of how my life continued to swirl in the same chaotic pattern for 10 years. But those 10 years made me appreciate life way more than the deadlines I set. Sometimes life happens and we must know that it's okay to go through those waves. Learn from it and evolve.

CROWN OF REJECTION

Reject: fail to show due affection or concern for (someone); rebuff.

Growing up, I knew I was destined for greatness. I could feel it in my being and would often dream about the success I wanted. Being the youngest sibling, you would think I was spoiled rotten, but I spent most of my days feeling alone with no one to relate to when I wanted. I was raised in a single parent home as I watched my mother work and take care of me the best she could. My mom married at a young age and had my two older sisters. When things went sour in her marriage, my biological dad came to the rescue. My parents found comfort in each other while they were experiencing problems in their personal lives. But when she was pregnant with me, he abandoned her. Then, my stepdad (my sisters' Dad) took me as his own and became my God Father. Even though God had a ram in the bush, I was still focused on having a bond with my biological father.

At a young age, I met the first obstacle that would alter the way I addressed situations and relationships. That hindrance was the fear of being REJECTED. The desire to be accepted made me vulnerable to seek any form of attention that filled the void of his absence. My Dad became the first void I tried to have men satisfy. He only came around on three occasions: Back to school shopping, Birthday celebrations, and Christmas mornings where he would faithfully drop off my gifts and rush to his unknown world. He was like a mystery I could never solve and when I would ask him personal "let me get to know you" questions, he would leave my emotions stranded in an ocean of uncertainty of my importance to his life. Those negative responses made me feel I was not good enough to be let into the secret places in his heart.

But the ram in the bush was my Godfather/Stepfather. I had his heart despite our genetic ties. He was not perfect but his love for me was. Although I accepted him as my father, I wanted to reverse the feeling of knowing that my biological father did not see me or want me as his own. Later in my teenage years, I found out I had other siblings. One day, I received a message on social media from a young woman who told me to call her. In that conversation, I discovered she was my older sister and was also told about my other siblings I was not fortunate to grow up with. I felt betrayed, but I began developing a bond as each one individually reached out to me. My first and only Christmas I spent at my Dad's house was after my newfound brother invited me over. Walking through my Dad's big house that had a pool, and a basketball court at the back made me hate him for all the times I wanted to be a part of his luxurious world. There were so many secrets I wanted to have the inside scoop on.

The spirit of rejection began to take root in my heart and was watered by my mother.

To make it worse, my mother wasn't the nurturing and affectionate type. Sometimes life hits us so hard that we place ourselves on autopilot and do the best to survive day by day. I feel my mom had to do what was needed to survive while taking the emotional aspect out of it. Rejection was a generational curse that played a part in my mother's life and she somehow carried over into mine. See, the devil is very tactful. Although he tries new things, he often goes back through generational ties to see if you would struggle with the same thing your parents and lineage wasn't able to persevere in the past.

Although I understand her now as a mother, we did not always see eye to eye as a teenager. My mother's love language was Acts of Service as Gary Chapman would describe in The 5 Love Languages Book. Her Sunday meals, buying new clothes for me, and fixing my hair was the love she could give at her capacity. But at the time as a teen, I needed quality time, words of affirmation, and physical touch as Gary Chapman explained to validate who I was. Growing up, my mother hardly told me she loved me. Hugs were not a common ordeal, and the only quality time we had together was watching American Idol auditions and laughing at the people who thought they could sing. I tried understanding her but the rejection from my dad made the lack of attention from my mother seem extreme. I wanted a certain type of love from my mother and a specific type of love from my father, which made me want a certain type of love from a mate.

TAINTED CROWN

Taint: to contaminate or pollute.

My first high school boyfriend was very kindhearted and affectionate. I had just finished performing my first theater performance in high school and was greeted with a teddy bear and a smile. He was very caring. Sometimes he would carry my backpack and books and walk me to class, risking being late to his. Our love was pure and we both respected each other's request to keep our innocence until marriage. I knew about sex from peers, but I was in no rush to have the experience because of my personal relationship with God.

Being a teen and finally receiving the attention I desired, all I wanted to do was give him all my time and attention. So, one day I snuck him over to my house when my mom was at work. I would regularly sneak neighborhood friends into my mother's home to rid me of boredom, but this was the first time I was sneaking a boy into our house. When he walked through my gate, a neighbor noticed him and called my mom to report me. Although our behaviors were innocent, the fact that he was alone with me in my mom's house was a problem. But as teenagers, I just desired a male's presence and wanted it by all means necessary. This was the beginning of a pattern I was springing forth by having guys fill the absence of my biological father.

Minutes later, my mom called me and sounded so furious on the phone. Immediately, I rushed him out of my home due to the fear that had already gripped me. My mother told me to get dressed and be ready to get in the car when she pulled up. The ride in the car was silent and being unaware of where we were heading made it even more awkward. We arrived at a hospital and my heart began to panic as I tried to figure out who was in the emergency room that we came to see. When the Clerk asked my mom, "How may I help you?" My mother responded,

"Yes, my daughter has been raped and I want to check to make sure she's okay!"

Staggering through my thoughts of the curveball that was just thrown, I assured the nurse that the serious accusation was false. Negating my claim, the nurses asked me to undress for an examination. I'm not sure if my mother was just punishing me or wanted to know if my virginity was still intact, but the allegation really affected me and my future decisions. I was sitting on the hospital bed with tears flowing down my face, trying to assure my mother and nurse that I had never been sexually involved with anyone. My mother smirked while the nurse began to treat me like a victim that was trying to protect their abuser. I was upset that my mother would make a claim that would not only affect me but could affect a young black boy who was completely innocent.

Days later, I came home from school to find STD and sex pamphlets lying on my bed, instead of an appropriate mother-daughter sex talk. I just remember thinking, "Wow, is this supposed to be the sex talk from my mom? Instead of talking to me, you avoid me and throw sex brochures on my bed". If anything, I learned more about sex from friends who were sexually active. After days of being accused of fornication, I told myself at 16 years old, "If I'm going to be accused of having sex every day and get weird looks and attitudes, WHY NOT JUST DO IT!" I started preparing myself for the next time I saw my boyfriend because IT was going to happen. That day after school, I told him what I wanted, and I could see the shock in his face and slight resistance in his body. He was fully aware of the situation that had occurred and was probably scared to follow through, but I had made up my mind and was tired of living a narrative that wasn't true. In the end, I lost my virginity that day. I opened the door for the devil to come right in to deepen wounds surrounding the rejection and mental abuse that was taking place internally. My high school boyfriend and I began arguing and cheating on each other. The pure and innocent love that we knew was now tainted by the door I opened out of revenge and pain. This created an "I'm going to get you first before you get me" attitude that lingered in my thoughts through adulthood. That relationship ended and the fear of being alone made me depressed all over again.

EMOTIONALLY ABUSED CROWN

Emotionally abused: any behavior that isn't physical, which may include verbal aggression, intimidation, and humiliation; often unfolds as a pattern of behavior over time that aims to diminish another's sense of identity, dignity, and self-worth.

Less than a year later, I met a freshman in college who I began to date. My high school is situated at a college campus and college courses were a part of my high school curriculum. So, I met a freshman in college while taking a class. Friendship led to a relationship and his words of affirmation and quality time temporarily filled the voids of rejection and lonesomeness. At home, I was denied the want to be seen and noticed and I became determined to find that in a relationship. We went to prom and began planning the next stages of our lives together. I finally graduated and instead of going to a university of my choice to study a 4-year college program, I settled for a community college. I was in no rush to leave my mother's home as my two older sisters did at eighteen years old. Things weren't at its best between my mother and me, but it was manageable. My eighteenth birthday came and it's as if my mom was suddenly reminded of the things my sisters did at eighteen, which I had to pay for. For days, my mom walked around the house deeply distraught and I couldn't understand why. She never expressed her true feelings but she continued to remind me of my sisters past mistakes as well as mine.

After ignoring my mother's unexpected mood swing for days, I came home to a long note attached to the refrigerator. I grabbed some juice, leaned against the counter and began reading the list of rules. I was now eighteen years old and was given an 8pm curfew If I was walking home. There was a 10pm curfew if I had a ride. I was only granted one hour to make phone calls on the house phone per day and could only text on my cell phone that she was paying for. There was a long list of rules but these rules made me feel imprisoned. It was as if my mom transformed fear into hatred of me being eighteen and possibly leaving the nest. Instead of showering me with love, she just pushed me further away with her strict rules. I found a job and complied to her rules.

One night after spending time with my boyfriend and mutual friends, I was given a ride home. I reached the front porch at ten o'clock on the dot. My boyfriend at the time requested to talk to my mom and apologized for bringing me home late. I remember telling my boyfriend how I did not want to go home because my mother was always angry and would do and say things to provoke a response. I was tired of mentally and emotionally fighting every day. It was as if a problem was made from everything and I suddenly was walking on eggshells in the house. He encouraged me to just put on my headphones and drown out the negative energy and do my best not to argue with her.

Trying my hardest to take his advice, I walked in the house and turned on the television and sat quietly. Minutes later, my mom began storming around the house and splashing anointing oil everywhere in anger. A little oil splashed on me and I wiped it off, talked myself into a calm state and continued watching TV. My mom grabbed the remote control, turned off the TV, cursed me out, and reminded me that she bought the TV I was watching. So, I walked fast and calmly towards my room with my headphones on just as my boyfriend advised me to when she asked me, "What spirit did you bring into my house?" Before I knew it, my mouth sprang opened and I started talking back. "What are you talking about?" My mom walked in her room, grabbed a bottle of olive oil (anointing oil) and drenched me, ruining my hair, spilling the oil all over my eyes and face and my clothes. We had a scuffle on my bedroom floor. I was unsure of where I would live but I knew I couldn't handle the abuse going from mental to spiritual. I was still a baby in Christ, and I couldn't handle someone treating me like I was a demon when I was trying my hardest to mold my life to others' expectations. I ran to a neighbor's house and broke down into tears. I called my boyfriend and explained what happened and he told me he would pick me up and that we were going to figure it out together.

IMMATURE CROWN

Immature: not fully developed.

Eighteen and fresh out of my mother's home, I was willing to risk it all with my newfound love. We began sleeping in abandoned cars together, warming up our bodies in the hot sun from the cold nights. Taking showers in his mother's home during the daytime and eating off McDonald's dollar menu almost every day. The struggle was very real and we started planning our future together. I was given a ring a month prior and we started discussing our marriage plans.

Word had circulated through my family of the situation that happened between my mother and I. My mom was spreading rumors that I was on drugs and had a pimp that was forcing me into whoredom behavior. I laughed it off, but it hurt that my mom would spread lies about me to alter my family's perception.

His mother helped us move into our own studio apartment

and bought us furniture. We started discussing marriage more often and started picking dates we would go to the courthouse and sign our marriage license. Although we were trying, we both were immature in what relationship entails and were moving way too fast. The need to continue to have him fill the void of lost love led me to do the worst thing any young woman could ever do. Scarred from rejection and fresh from mental abuse, I altered my entire world in effort to keep this man by any means necessary. I was unsure of who I truly was and what I wanted out of life, but I put so much energy into him while hindering my own growth. I stunted who I was evolving to become to put my energy in developing my newfound guy into who he was becoming. I lost my identity while helping him find his own. The closer he reached that goal, the more we grew apart and his heart began to grow cold.

At the time, we attended Bible study groups with young adults around the same age as us. The more we bonded with the leader of the Bible study group, the more his true character began to stand out. One time while hanging at his home, the group leader had a woman over who I believe he was dating at the time. While we were lightly conversing, the lady friend began to voice her opinion. The group leader looked over at her in a calm but stern tone and asked, "Did I give you permission to speak?" The lady friend stopped talking and sat back as if she was a fly on the wall the entire time we stayed there. The man I loved started hanging out more with the group leader and slowly began adopting his behavior. He would ask me questions and stop mid-sentence reassuring himself that since I was a woman, I wouldn't know the answer. He began devaluing me as a person due to my gender. We were no longer equal, instead I was now seen as a servant to his liking. I was now being treated like the "lady friend" which led to arguments over silly things. In the studio apartment, there was hardly anywhere to go but the bathroom, kitchen, or outside to sit on the steps to cool off.

The day finally came and my gut was on full blast. I could not shake the feeling throughout the day that he would call it quits. I told a few friends and they brushed it off saying I was just panicking and overthinking. But one thing I have learned is to always trust your gut. For most women, when we have an intuition, it's not that we are crazy, rather it simply means that God is preparing us for what's going to happen next in our lives and for us to recognize what type of people are in our midst.

When I went home, he asked me to join him for a stroll through the neighborhood park. He not only broke up with me but kicked me out of the apartment. I felt abandoned again and the fear of being alone and rejected resurfaced. I invested all of myself into this relationship and didn't even know who I was or how to move forward. I played the silly woman for a while, and would visit him, cook for him, clean the house without his knowledge, and even continued intimacy with him. But one night after we had sex, he received a phone call around midnight from a woman. I wasn't alarmed that he received the phone call, but I felt disrespected that he decided to answer the phone while still lying naked beside him in bed. Overhearing the short conversation while staring in the bathroom mirror, I had to reassure myself that I deserved better. That next morning, I got up and shook the dust.

At the time, I was now living with two male roommates. While walking the college campus, God introduced me to a woman who would become my spiritual mentor. It was as if God had rescued me and He began to take His time to mend my broken heart. When we are brokenhearted, our bodies suffer greatly. Our serotonin levels are altered and the stress and sadness begin to shift our thoughts. But God rescued me from that, acknowledging me as His own and guiding me daily. I would be in church 3 to 4 times a week and things began looking good for me. I found a new job, my mother and I finally reconciled and I moved back in with her, and I even heard God's voice. I started learning about God and began to apply it into my daily walk.

CROWN OF BITTERNESS

Bitterness: anger and disappointment of being treated unfairly; resentment.

One night, I had a dream that I was begging my sisters to take me to my stepdad before he died. Less than a week after I had the dream, I received a phone call that he was sick but refused to go to the doctor for a checkup. Being a veteran of the Vietnam war, his anxiety was well understood.

My sisters and I went to his house and begged him to go to the doctor, and we assured him that everything was going to be okay. After his appointment, I received a phone call that the man I knew as my Dad was sick with cancer. He was diagnosed with esophageal cancer and it had spread to his lungs, liver and brain.

I prayed without ceasing and believed that God would heal my daddy. I didn't let the negative talk of him dying infiltrate my thoughts because I learned so much about faith and I had to activate it to save my father. My sister took care of him every step of the way, praying with him, reading scriptures and encouraging him to keep the faith.

We were called to the hospital to watch him take his last breath. I remember staring at my dad on his sickbed struggling to breathe, while I talked to God in my mind and asked Him to save him.

There were moments in my life that I had not shared with my Dad yet. I wanted my father to walk me down the aisle and give me away to be married. I wanted my dad to hold his future grandkids in his arms and share his smile, stories, and jokes with them. I wanted my children to show him their report cards and receive the reward of a dollar for every A and bargain for more money just like me. I wanted my mate to hear the threat that if he mistreated me, all my dad needed was one bullet, not to kill him but to get him real good where he'll remember the experience for the rest of his life. When the machine flatlined, so did my faith in God. I tried to believe that maybe God would surprise me and perform a miracle and bring him back, but after I danced at his funeral and touched his casket, I knew that was the last moment I was going to share with him. After the many tears I shed at his funeral, anger and bitterness began taking root, next to rejection and abuse.

I never doubted God was real, but I began to feel that maybe He did not care about me. I began to feel inadequate as a child of God, thinking that maybe I was undeserving of love and happiness especially from the male species. The rejection of my request made me think that perhaps, God saw me as a stepchild. Rejected from my biological dad, disappointed and abused by my mother, and abandoned by my ex-fiancé, I became bitter and enraged that God was serving me a taste of all three medicines that began taking root and growing steady.

A person willing to make a relationship work past disappointment would have sought God for answers, asked for strength and encouragement, and tried to stay connected to Him. But being a baby in Christ and immature in thought, I allowed this stumbling block to take me off course completely. People think that when you start your faith walk that everything will be like skipping through roses and tulips all day long. But just like any relationship, mother-daughter, sister-brother, husband-wife, God-servant, there will be unexpected turns, good times, as well as the bad. Any old couple willing to offer relationship advice would gladly tell you that there were moments that they questioned their relationship. But I was so focused on the end of my relationship with my stepdad that I stopped focusing on my relationship with my Creator. When they would tell me to keep the faith while I'm in the church, I would think, "I tried that and look at what happened to my dad!" When they would say God knows the desires of my heart, it pissed me off even more because I knew that He knew my desire but did not grant it. When I heard the scriptures of God meeting every need, all I could think of was the need of feeling and desiring love.

I felt that my relationship with God was a waste of time. I had turned a deaf ear to my spirituality and vowed to myself that I would no longer be the Christian Jessica and would do whatever I wanted to do at any cost.

My church attendance went from 3-4 times a week to now 1-2. The promise I made to God pertaining to celibacy was out the window. I wanted to feel something other than pain, and

27

the best immediate revenge towards God was to give my body to someone even for a momentary pleasure.

I had my mind set on the type of person I wanted to give my body to. I pretty much did the devil's homework and I'm sure he was excited to set me up with the right person per my request. I had walked away from my safety net with God to set up a business meeting with the devil on how he could destroy my life. I had left my father's house like the prodigal son from a misunderstanding. And I had to pay for this decision for the years ahead.

CROWN OF ILLUSION

Illusion: a thing that is or is likely to be wrongly perceived or interpreted by the senses; a deceptive appearance or impression; a false idea or belief.

While walking the community college campus, I met a guy who caught my attention. He was charming and crafty with his words. His responses were clever and his body language was self-assured. I wanted the strength he exemplified and had casted him in this imaginary role that I would later bring to his attention.

Over time, we exchanged numbers and I made it crystal clear that my intentions were solely sex. I planned to eventually work up to have as many guys as the days of the week. Feeding my lustful desires, I made him my "Tuesday night guy" in which we would meet, have sex, leave, and repeat the cycle every Tuesday evenings. I felt like I had taken some control in my life, orchestrating meaningless sex with him while treating him like a stranger on campus. Still, I did not want to lose sight of my heartless purpose because I knew that once my heart got involved, it would mess up my plan.

On a day other than Tuesday, I received a call from him inviting me over for a movie. My woman's curse just started and I was in no shape to play "woman of the night".

"Why is everything with you about sex? Why can't we just enjoy each other's company?"

"Fine I'll come over."

While cuddling and watching movies, the door to my emotions swung wide open, leaving my whoredom plan to subside. What was potentially just a movie and cuddle session for him was an oasis of emotions that suddenly sprung up in my heedless desert. Notwithstanding the number of times I spoke to my emotions to calm down and think logically, I was caught up in the fantasy and the feelings of lust that made me feel it was love.

My feelings grew stronger for this man and before I knew it, I was committed to spending nights at his house 3-4 times a week as I previously was in church. His place began to feel more of a comfort space and peace of mind than living with my mother, as my heartless actions started taking a toll on our mother-daughter relationship. I had the illusion that we would soon be in a relationship until I came across a picture of another woman. When I confronted him, he admitted being in a relationship with another woman and claimed that he was caught in "a love triangle." He asked me not to leave and to give him time to fix things. Days later, he convinced me that he ended that relationship and wanted me to stay around. He made it seem that he was developing feelings for me. We started spending more time together and sharing highlights of our lives before we met.

His father passing during his teen years was the tactful scheme the devil used to get me emotionally invested. Seeing the vase that his father's ashes sat in brought back the pain of losing my stepfather, and I felt that this man could understand me deeper than anyone. His father's ashes justified my emotions that maybe we were meant to be together since that was the sole reason I turned from God in the first place. And I began giving him access to me while expecting him to fill the voids and heal the wounds of my past. His attention gave me comfort. The sex was a temporary fill to the absence of the previous men that rejected me. Eventually, all the energy I put into being careless was now invested into him. I let him into my inner space and made him my priority.

I was now fixated and wasting so much thought and energy on him. We went on a few dates but I understood I was not the only girl he was spending his quality time with. I would see his caller ID with names that I knew he was intimate with. But I was determined to make the illusion of him being my man become a reality even if that meant practically moving in with him. I was persuaded that he was the only human being on the face of the earth that had the ability to put my mind at ease, and I gave him full power to do so. However, the intimacy made me grow weaker as I felt at times our bodies were floating in space. I was what some may call it as being "dickmatized." Some things are only great in our lives because we give power to it.

My coworkers started suspecting I was pregnant and I shoved it off until one morning I woke up and could barely move due to the tenderness in my breast. I stopped by the drug store and picked up a pregnancy test to silence the thoughts that my coworkers poisoned me with. The first test immediately revealed the pink positive sign but I was not convinced. I felt that maybe the test was defective or perhaps, I misread the instructions or wrongfully angled it. After reading the instructions over twice, I persisted with the second test as if I was trying to pass a final exam in college. A plus sign appeared on the second test and my mouth instantly dropped open while tears streamed down my face. My heart pounded out of my chest as I made THE call during my lunch break to tell him about my pregnancy. My nerves were jumping everywhere because I feared what his response would be.

"So, you think that just because you took a test, that means you're pregnant?"

What type of response was that?

"Well, I actually took two. I am going to the emergency after work to confirm the results. You can meet me there if you want."

His response told me everything I needed to know. I was not about to raise a baby in an imperfect household. I always told myself that I wanted to be married before birthing a child. As I walked to the train to get to the doctor's office, I couldn't help but shed a few tears as I began to apologize to my unborn child. My phone began to ring and behold, it was my mentor calling and she had prophesied about this destruction if I kept walking down this path in my life. It took everything in me to not answer the phone but I wanted to be comforted just by her voice alone. God began to reveal my pregnancy to her and she spoke blessings over my unborn child's life. Just like that, my mindset shifted and I knew that I couldn't go against what God had approved to be here.

The doctor confirmed my pregnancy and the drive back home was quiet. Days went by and we avoided discussing the elephant in the room. It was as if we had never discovered I was pregnant, but my body and mind couldn't go back to normalcy. So, I made an appointment with my doctor and I asked him to drive me since I was a few weeks from finishing my driving school lessons. The morning came and I tried numerous times to wake him up but to no avail. I shook him before I got out of bed, called his name after I showered, and yelled at him after getting dressed. I could tell at some point that he was pretending to be asleep to avoid taking me. Furious that he purposely made me miss my appointment, I went into the kitchen and filled a pot with cold water and poured it on him. He slowly rose to his feet, walked over to his dresser, and grabbed a belt. He threw me to the ground and whipped me like a child. After he was done, he dropped the belt and held me as I cried for him to let me go. I began packing my bags to leave as he followed me around with sorrowful eyes. As I stood at the front door with my bags packed, it was as if my feet began to melt into the ground. I stood there, staring outside the front door, unable to take the next steps to walk out. I was afraid of being a single parent, especially the fear of repeating what I had gone through as a child. My lingering fear of being rejected and alone convinced me to drop my bags and give it another try. He held me and apologized with kisses on my cheeks. I felt that because he apologized, somehow things would get better but I was wrong. Things kept going up and down.

Jessica Simington

The pregnancy took a heavy toll on my body. He had to rush me to the emergency room a few times but although he was there, he wasn't supportive nor had compassion. I remember picking up my prescriptions from the pharmacy, and when I turned around from the counter, all my discharge papers were scattered on the floor. Sick as a dog, I had to get on my knees with my baby bump trying to put all the papers into one big pile and catch up with him on the way to the car. I was so embarrassed, but instead of removing myself from him, I continued to stay there and take the treatment at the cost of momentary attention.

I picked up some items to help me get through my morning sickness. Every black mama has a routine for their sick child and I knew exactly what my mom would do to make me feel better. One morning, he was being extra nice to me and made me soup and kissed me goodbye while he went to work. I was too sick to eat and just wanted to rest. His brother woke me up from my sleep and advised me to eat my soup before it got cold. I took his advice, and a couple of hours later, I put a spoon full in my mouth and immediately spat it out. I found enough strength to go into the bathroom and flush the soup down the toilet so everyone could leave me alone and believe that I ate it. While pouring it out, as I got closer to the last portion of the soup in the bowl, I found a bad attempt of crushed pills floating around the bottom of the bowl. Immediately, I knew that the reason he came home late that night had to do with his plans of wanting me to have a miscarriage from the food he served me, but it failed. I asked him about it and he denied ever putting anything in the soup.

I rushed to the emergency room after that and my mom

came to the hospital on a mission. She was concerned and picked me up from the emergency room to take me home for a couple of days. Days grew into weeks and my sickness worsened. I was now closely monitored with an in-home nurse that would medicate me and change my IV fluids daily.

BATTERED CROWN

Battered: injured; having suffered repeated violence from a spouse, partner, or parent.

I eventually regained my strength after the hectic first trimester and the first place I rushed to be was his house. I was determined to make a family work and would do anything it took to not feel the rejection and lonesomeness that trailed me my entire life. When I went back, everything suddenly seemed better than before. He was happy to see me when he got home. He was communicating and he finally started treating me like the girlfriend I desired to be. Things were looking great until one day I walked into the living room and a female was laying on the couch under a blanket. She introduced herself as his best friend and I got to find out that she didn't have a place to live and was staying there temporarily. What was looking and feeling like a honeymoon gradually turned into a nightmare. We began fighting over Miss Best friend and her actions which

I felt were disrespectful. I would come home from work and they would be cuddled up next to each other on our bed. One day, he was taking a shower and she opened the door to get advice on the two lingerie outfits she picked out for her first night dancing at the strip club. Boundaries were being crossed and arguments were the new normal as he made me feel I was blowing things out of proportion.

Heated text messages spilled over into the night. I had a gut feeling that something bad was going to happen, so I called my cousin to let her know I was coming over for the night. After I packed my bags, I talked myself out of leaving to get some rest and perhaps leave in the morning. I laid in the bed wide awake when he bust through the door. I could smell the alcohol on his breath as he propped me on my back, sat on top of me and urged me to talk. I was mentally drained from the argument that carried on throughout the day and just wanted to go to bed. He began to make comments indicating that he would harm me so I wouldn't have the baby. I became terrified as he put more body weight on me to prevent me from going away from his assaults. I asked if I could go to the restroom so I could try to escape out of the bathroom window, but he followed me there and the window grew smaller in my eyes. I tried to calculate my next move. There were two exits from his bedroom. One door led to the backyard of the house, which meant I have to walk around to get out of the front gate. And the other door led through the house to the front door. I stared into his eyes and they were emotionless. After washing my hands, I opened the door and began running out of the room. I passed his siblings' bedrooms to the front door to hopefully get outside and to find anybody that could help me. But he chased me, picked me up, dragged me back to the bedroom and locked the door.

Hours went by and I was certain that the alcohol had worn off. Our conversation started to change direction and he suggested that we both go to sleep as he locked me in his arms. I thought that maybe since he was in a sober mood, I could get some rest. I woke up to him lifting me off the bed and supernaturally, the song "God Blocked It" by Kurt Carr began to blast in my ear. There was a blanket laid out on the floor and he gently laid me on the blanket.

"God Blocked It."

He sat on my chest with his back facing me and began punching my stomach. I started screaming and kicking while the song continued to blast in my ears.

"God Blocked It."

Punch after punch, I cried out hoping that someone would hear me. A few moments later, I heard someone break open the door and try to pull him off me, but his strength overpowered his brothers. His brother stormed out the room defeated in his attempt.

"God Blocked It."

The door was wide open and I could see his sister on the phone making a call. His mother walked in and told him to stop because he could kill me. He stopped momentarily and said, "Do you want to watch?" With that being said, he resumed his steady punches. As my strength began to wear off along with my hope for the baby, Cops entered both sides of the house. I was hit with an abundance of questions and after answering majority of them, all I wanted was to get to the emergency room to see if my baby was alive. When I got to the hospital, tears began to form and I could see the fear in the nurse's eyes as she placed the gel on my stomach. My baby's heart was beating and I was in disbelief as to how it was possible after the beating I got from him. It was as if an angel had placed a speaker to my right ear and pressed the play button to "God Blocked It" to assure me that whatever plan he had in mind wasn't going to succeed.

Someone once stated: "When God shows you it's time to let someone go and you refuse to, He will allow the person to hurt you to the point you have no choice but to let go." (Anonymous)

God was trying to detach me time and time again from the abusive relationship but I did not heed to the warning. So now, I was left dealing with the consequences of my own actions while God still showed me love and gave me a way of escape.

The nurse came back to discharge me and asked me for a number to call so I would be picked up. I was without my phone and the only number I could think about was my mother's number. So I called her and explained what happened since I couldn't hide the scars.

Hours went by from the time I called my mother to pick me up and I knew that every one of my family members was current on the recent news. You would think that a mother would wrap her arms around her hurting child, instead I was yelled at as if it was all my fault. She walked around upset and disappointed and it poured salt on the new wounds as well as the old ones from the past.

Arguments arose every day. We even argued several times walking through the courthouse to address the domestic violence I went through. I had no support and it hurt when my mother said the one thing a mother should never say to a child fresh out of abuse.

"If I was him, I would have beat your ass too."

The argument had gone too far and I cried for days behind my mother negligence. After his sister came to my house and begged me not to report her brother and have him locked up, my mom asked me to drop the charges and not send another black boy to jail. Tired of my phone ringing every second with questions and traveling back and forth to the court, I convinced myself to write a letter. With my letter in hand, the two cops that spoke with me on that night hopped on the elevator with me and my mom. They asked me what I had decided to do about the situation and I told them I was going to drop the charges. The cops were disappointed because this is a normal habit surrounding victims of abusive relationships in urban communities. My mother began to take sides with the police as if I came up with this decision on my own. I felt hurt and betrayed and I told myself that I would rather be hit by a man than to continue to be mentally abused by my mother. The evidence was so bad that the judge was lost for words but because my letter was professionally written, the judge decided to allow the charges to be dropped.

Finally, I went back to work and all the other black women there began telling me their abusive stories with their husbands and boyfriends. Here, I was thinking I was the odd ball as I sat among a community of black women who had convinced me that physical abuse was the normalcy of every real relationship. One after the other, they shared their stories and high fives were exchanged when reciting their revengeful schemes on how they planned to get them back.

"Girl, if he didn't love you, he would have never put his

hands on you. He's mad because his love for you is growing out of control and men like to be in control. Just teach him a lesson to not do it again and you'll be fine."

The devil is so tactful that even while God is trying to give you a way out, he already drafts a plan to suck you right in. Whenever I looked forward to doing good, evil was always present, raising its ugly head to fight my decisions. (Reference to Romans 7:21) The longing to be loved, to be seen, and to be noticed was now validated from the advice of these women. I went right back to my abuser because I wanted to take my chances on love and not continue to live in a home where my feelings were being damaged further from mental and emotional abuse. I opened the door back up and we began talking. Notwithstanding what I went through in his hand during pregnancy, I gave birth to a healthy baby girl.

CROWN OF INSANITY

Insanity: extreme foolishness; folly; senselessness. Some may say it's doing the same thing and expecting different results.

I was determined to have the image of a complete family, even if it was toxic. My mother was disappointed that I had a child out of wedlock and I could feel it every day from her actions and spoken words. Can you guess what I did next? You are correct. He called me and asked if he could take me out on a date. I got ready and he picked me up to go dancing. We were gleaning with smiles and long gazes that night. After a few slow dances, tight grips, and hands being held, I moved right back in a few days later. Things were looking good as the cycle always started and then our first argument happened. I immediately shut my mouth, reliving the trauma and he would walk away to take long walks in order to control his anger. But most of those long walks resulted in me lying in an empty bed in a cold room all by myself.

August 26th – Day after my birthday and he's back to his regular routine of disappearing when issues arise. He's not picking up the phone, no text messages to keep me posted, no telling me where he went the next day, No nothing. I'm very pissed off right now.

August 27th – I'm not really expecting him to come back. I'm over texting and begging for attention. Two days before my staged performance, so I need to stay focused.

Sept 2nd - Poem of the Day

I'm not perfect, but there are times I need to self-reflect
All the hurtful times and disrespect is building up inside,
heavy pressure in my chest
I'm not perfect,
but the reciprocation has been a constant imperfection
The want and need for love are only a suggestion
Cause my generation is dumb to stoop low
for love and affection
Blind sighted to correction, unlearned lessons
Same seat, same class, learning the same lessons
I'm not perfect, school bell rings and I'm in the same classes.
When am I going to learn?

Someone said the devil sits back and takes note on ways to keep us bound. I'm certain that this is true because every time I set my mind on leaving, he would come home from days of being away with his crafty words and convincing notions. His absence would create arguments that led to sex, which eventually lead me back in the same position of not wanting to leave. Jonathan McReynolds has a song called "Cycles" where he states: "The devil, he learns from your mistakes, even if you don't. That's how he keeps you in cycle"

Someone else said that insanity is doing the same thing and expecting different results. I was in a cycle that eventually led to my second pregnancy. Trauma was suddenly revisited as arguments thickened. And now, we were taking trips to the abortion clinics that ended in me having anxiety and panic attacks. I was once again attending doctor appointments alone and hiding my prenatal pills.

Eventually, the conversation of me terminating my pregnancy became the main topic of every discussion we had. The excuse of not having enough money came into play and even the ultimatum of him ending our relationship became the forefront of the result of not terminating the pregnancy.

"See the way my heart is set up; I only have the capacity to love so many people. And there's only one space in my heart left. If you choose to get rid of the baby then you will fill that space. But if you choose to keep the baby then only that baby can fill that space. But I can't love you both, so you have to choose."

The pep talks became alarming and mind bothering, and so I agreed to visit an abortion clinic to make him happy. I just wanted everything to go away. When I arrived at Planned Parenthood, they refused to service me stating that I was medically insured by my biological father. That was the first and only time I felt that my biological father had done something right on my behalf. After calling the insurance company, I was told that my designated medical facility was in the heart of Lancaster. So, we picked a day to drive out and we finally arrived at the hospital.

Even more, I was shocked that he took the drive to Lancaster. He took more time taking me to abortion clinics than going to the doctor's office. His persistence made me want the nightmare to be over. My name was eventually called and I walked to the back to see an older nurse waiting for me. She went through the normal pregnancy pre-check questions and when she asked me what brought me in today, I answered that I wanted to know more about my options.

Then she said to me, "I was just about to go home today and I asked for one more patient."

She asked me why, and I told her about my baby daddy was pressuring me to remove the unborn child. She shared her story with me about how she was pressured to have an abortion. Everything she said started to make sense to me and I was even shocked it was all happening. I was just a week away from abortions to be illegal in the state of California.

"We nurses can always give the wrong estimate of your due date. I'm going to go ahead and document you as being one week ahead, making it illegal to do anything. And when you go into that office, you just tell the doctor that you just wanted a regular checkup. I'm going to give you your paperwork and you tell your baby daddy that it's too late for you to do anything!"

I felt that she was a guardian angel sent by God to save me from my illusion. He was so mad at the news as I sat in the passenger seat and kept smiling inside. We got back to his place and his disappearing acts began to surface again. But I was unbothered and just enjoyed the peace and comfort I felt in his home as I was surrounded by his family.

Closer to the due date of my second child, more situations began to arise. My children's grandmother suffered from a certain mental illness. Because I refused to drink milk and to give my infant whole milk, she called Child Protective Services and told them that I was not feeding my child. The investigator that was assigned to come over to me advised me to get some paperwork signed and return them to him so that the case can be closed.

The same day that I turned in the paperwork to the investigator was the same day I found out that my baby daddy was seeing another woman. So, I packed up my belongings, left some damage behind and went to hide at my Aunt's house in case he came looking for me. He blew up my phone the entire day and I finally gave in and told him where I was. He asked me if I could come outside to talk and I convinced my cousin to go with me as my daughters slept on their portable beds. As I walked towards the father of my children, he dragged me across the lawn, ripping my housecoat into shredded pieces. He dragged me to the back stairs of the apartment and sat me down and said, "Now we can talk."

This violent act led to the cops being called, my mom being tormented by them making a stop at her house afterwards, and a fully open case with Child Protective Services by Monday morning.

The courts were involved yet again and I was deemed as an unfit parent who was being victimized. I had to take parenting classes, domestic violence for victims, and counseling to prove myself as a mother. I already had so much on my plate but I knew I had to make this work this time. I was working, attending College, taking care of my one-year old and 3-week-old baby. I was stressed trying to find time and money to attend classes while finding a babysitter. My life gradually became impossible and the illusion I was creating of this perfect family was fully shattered. I didn't know what to do and I was tired of the chaos that followed me.

CROWN OF RAGE

Rage: violent; uncontrollable anger.

The day after I had just given birth to my second daughter, I was visited by my mother.

"Is this all you're going to do with your life?"

"Ma this is not the time to have this conversation. "

"I must have done a terrible job as a parent. I'm so disappointed in you."

I was afraid that everyone in the hospital heard her comments and after she stormed out of my room, the nurse came in and asked if I was okay. That was so embarrassing and mind-boggling that she couldn't wait until I at least got home. Arguments between my mother and I was going too far. My newborn was just a month old when she kicked me out of her house. I moved in with a friend in her studio apartment. I went to school in the morning between 8am-12pm, made it to work from 2pm-11pm, and went to my friend's studio apartment where I slept with my children on the floor. And between those hours in the day, I was calling around trying to enroll in classes to prove myself as a parent. Social workers were making routine visits, and to read the reports of what she gathered was even more upsetting.

My mother and I began talking after a few months. I had initially planned to spend the night at her house, but when we started arguing, I gathered my belongings and packed up. As I was taking a trip to load my car, my mom closed the door and locked me outside of the house. I banged on the door, demanding that she opens it, but there was no response. I just couldn't believe that the only control I had left of being a mother was now being tested as I was locked outside of her house. I had so much anger in me and all the buried pain began to rise once again. I was at my breaking point feeling that everything in my life was spiraling downhill. She dropped them off at their daycare, and while picking them up, I received a phone call from one of my social workers stating that my mother called in and told them I abandoned my kids and she would want them to live with her. Tears began to flow from my eyes that my own mother would betray me. I explained that I did not abandon my children but was locked out of the house. It was one thing after another and I just couldn't bear to take it anymore. I didn't talk or visit my mother for an entire year after the incident. In the midst of those challenges, I tried to contact my dad but he was intentionally avoiding my phone calls.

Visits between children were now being exchanged at a police station and not only was I handing my baby over to him, I was handing them over to his new girlfriend whom he had just moved in with and was pregnant as well. I was fed up.

Every day that passed by, I felt there was something new to discover or deal with. I felt like I was in the middle of the ocean and once I caught my breath from a vicious wave, there was another wave awaiting me to swallow me.

I was now angry and was plotting in revengeful schemes. One night, I constructed a plan that I would pour sugar down my baby daddy's gas tank. I had the pack of sugar in my car and was waiting for the time I knew he would be at work. Somehow, I got distracted from the plan and later that night when he called me, he told me that his car just happened to stop on its own while he was driving. I knew God was trying to tell me:

"I will take revenge; I will pay them back. In due time their feet will slip. Their day of disaster will arrive, and their destiny will overtake them." (Deut 32:35 NLT)

But I felt that God was taking too long and I had to take matters into my own hands. I wanted to hurt him so badly for everything that transpired throughout the time he came into my life. I wanted him to pay for playing with my emotions and leaving me to defend myself alone, and for not wanting to be with me or to share the image I created in my head of a "happy family." I had become Melinda from Tyler Perry's movie Acrimony. I had a strong hate and the devil kept suggesting things I should do right in my ear. The only thing that kept me distracted from fulfilling half of the suggestions was being busy with school, children, work, and theatrical performances. God kept me busy to keep my mind off the ideas I had planned. I knew things went too far when I was planning on how to burn down the apartment building he resided in with his new family. When I fully planned out the entire scenario, I could feel God telling me that I would be in jail if I didn't stop.

When we take revenge into our own hands, we take the responsibility away from God. The Bible says it's okay to be angry, but to sin not. (Ephesians 4:26). I was about to create a huge crime that would have made the life I was working so hard for be in vain. So, I gave it to God and gazed at another crown. I started thinking that maybe I should end my own life because it became too hard for me to handle.

SUICIDAL CROWN

Suicide: the act of intentionally causing one's own death.

My world was out of control and I didn't know where to start to put my pieces back together. I had taken a long walk through a cold and dark tunnel where there was no light at the end. I thought that this was how my life was going to be forever. I began to convince myself that maybe my children would be okay without a mother who was mentally all over the place. So, I started contemplating suicide. I was tempted by prescription pills, stared at sharp knives in the kitchen, and was focused on anything that posed a threat to my life. Depression had overtaken me and I wanted to end the continual feeling of heartbreak and internal agony. I was deeply distressed about every relationship that I desired love from. I felt that I had no control over my life and every time I went to pick up my pieces, something else around me would shatter. The only thing that kept me somewhat sane was my acting career in staged play productions. Reading scripts filled with drama temporarily took me out of that state of mind and kept me together.

One day after a photo shoot for a production, I had just watched an episode of "Being Mary Jane" and was inspired by how Mary's friend, Lisa, committed suicide. I was dressed up, hair done, make-up done and was debating whether to drive into something as I was parked with my engine still running. I was completely zoned out and had just made peace with my decision when my phone started going off. People were blowing my phone up left and right and the buzzing began interfering with my concentration. It's like God kept taking me out of that state of mind and drew my focus in on the phone. The person who had driven me to make this rash decision was now blowing me up along with his sister. I picked up the phone thinking that maybe I could give him my last words of anger, but was startled when my baby daddy answered in a panic. He was worried and said he had awakened from a dream where I kissed my kids goodbye and walked out in traffic on the freeway. He called his sister when I wouldn't answer and they took turns calling me until I answered the phone. I felt a cold chill run through my body at those words he said to me. I just couldn't understand why God wanted me to live in this tornado of chaos.

One Sunday night, my church had a youth event where singers came with worship music and the altar was open for anyone who wanted to share. A young girl in her early teens came forward with her poems. After reciting her first poem, she began reciting a second poem she recently wrote as a letter to a person that wanted to commit suicide. Every word that came out of that young girl's mouth was as if God gave her the words to talk directly to me. I began to tear up and it touched my heart. That night, I decided that I would cease the idea of ending my life. As stated, "Why end your full life over a temporary situation?" You never know if tomorrow could have been your breakthrough. Why take that risk? This was all over a broken heart. God had to remind me that He's the one who heals the brokenhearted and bandages the wounds. (Psalm 147).

CROWN OF SELF-AWARENESS

Self-awareness: having conscious knowledge of one's own character and feelings.

After everything, I did exactly what the prodigal son did after coming to his senses. I ran back to my first love. I felt that I was losing my mind and God sent my mentor to reconnect me back to God spiritually, emotionally, and mentally. With her help, I eventually moved into family housing for battered women and children, and shared half a room with another family. We had strict rules that I hated then but appreciate now because it taught me balance and discipline where it was really needed. Some of the women in the house had been through tough paths worse than mine. It was God's way of telling me that everything was going to be okay.

My mind was drifting away due to the trauma and hurt I had experienced. My mentor would cry and ask me why some things weren't connecting for me mentally, and I remember telling her that I literally felt like my mind was floating in space. I had lost so much. I had instability in almost every relationship I encountered and the security of having my babies was almost jeopardized because I played the victim way too long.

Poem written in 2015

I'm scarred, feelings packed tight
Mentally drained and tired
Tired of the lies, the pain, the momentary "pick me ups"
To be dropped and unbothered
Feelings whooping my ass like a mob
Eyes sore from the tears that flow as I sob
All I want is someone to love my soul
But I keep singing the same sad love song
Am I not good enough? Am I not worthy?
Why is there never a happy ending to my love story?
Every door of my life has been coated with pain
Pretenders unmasked when they all were the same
Liars, abusers, heart stompers, and mind manipulators
Egos to be stroked, penis thinkers, selfish tailored
How much more of this can I take?
Move this plate, I already ate
And had this no substance and unfulfilling cake
I can't wait, stop talking, I seen this before
And I won't take the bait
Someone please save me
Save me with innocent intentions
Motives far from malicious
Add to me like interest

Save this wounded victim and end this war within me
I want to find rest and a still place.
I want to find me.

I was back in church and was constantly reading my Bible. Some days were extremely uncomfortable and I could feel God pruning spirits off me that I picked up along the way. Those first couple of months back in His presence was some of the hardest because I felt I was in spiritual bootcamp. I had to look back at everything I went through and find the root.

To heal, we have to go to the root of the issue. I had to acknowledge that God's ways are not our ways. I had to see my father's passing as God saving him from the pain he faced on his deathbed. It wasn't so much about me and my wants, just that it was my Father's time to go. God is fully aware that we will not understand everything and that it's okay to be mad, but just not to sin against Him. Because I sinned, I suffered. Walking away from God was the worst decision I ever made. I had less pain suffering behind my father's passing alone than everything I endured by wanting to do things my way. My way got me into a lot of mess that I asked God to clean up.

The idea that in order to come to God everything has to be perfect is a false religious perspective. Being a Christian doesn't mean that you are perfect, but striving toward perfection in your daily walk. Having a made-up mind to walk with God is what keeps you bonded with Him. I had to understand that a relationship with God was just like having a relationship with someone else. It takes work and most times, it's not an overnight fix. Every day is a growing experience to learn what pleases God and what doesn't. Despite my betrayal from God, He took His time to clean me up. He is the Potter and I am the clay and He started the process of putting molding me back together. (Reference Jeremiah 18:4). That alone is what real love is. This is a testament that you don't have to be perfect to come to God. Just come open-hearted and willing to seek after God and He will surely increase you. I began asking God who I am in Him, and one night, I awoke from a dream with a pencil ready to document what I just saw in my journal.

August 14th – I had a dream that I was in a photo with this armor on. I was laying down with a mic in my hand. Draped in Fine purple and trimmed with gold. I looked like Queen Sheba being carried on a throne. Everyone was staring at me. There I laid like a giant sitting in the four corners of the picture frame at an art gallery. I was a moving picture that everyone was staring in awe. It was beautiful. ☺

I was stopped by a prophet I hardly knew and he screamed when he saw me. He said I was in his dream a few days prior and here I was in the flesh standing before him. He got quiet and the next words that came out of his mouth stuck with me even until today.

"Young Lady, God said pick up YOUR Crown. You've forgotten who you are and where you come from. You are a King's kid. Pick it up and wear it proudly."

This was God revealing who I was and what I needed to correct. I was starting to find my purpose, which gave me hope. My life finally had meaning and I was finding happiness in my life again.

CROWN OF RESEMBLANCE

Resemble: having qualities or features; look or seem like.

I became focused on bettering myself that I tried my hardest not to focus on any man. I began meeting my relatives from my father's family as they reached out to get to know me. My Aunt told me that the reason my Dad was avoiding my phone calls was because he was disappointed that I had children.

"Well, maybe if he would have been there for me, then I wouldn't have had tolerated so much from men to fill his missing void."

I was trying my best to forgive my parents and anyone that had hurt me along the way. The scripture, to love others as you love yourself (Mark 12:31), had me thinking about the love yourself part. How could I love someone else if I didn't know who I was? I was on my journey seeking to know the real me, which somehow caught the attention of men. I started thinking that maybe men were attracted to women that mind their own business. Being a woman and having an eye for muscles, soft eyes, and a nice smile, I dated a few men and started creating my list of what I desired in a mate.

I met a fine guy that resembled many qualities on my list of a desirable mate. He was charming, well-dressed, well-mannered, an attention giver, and a gentleman pulling out chairs, opening car doors, handing me his coat when I was cold, and catered for me as a woman. We were talking almost every day, waking up to Good Morning text messages and even talked about God.

Soon, we were working together which granted us more quality time. I was fighting my feelings until we were both invited to a friend's social gathering. My children gravitated to him like a magnet. Sitting next to him quietly watching a movie, I sat back in amazement being that this was the first time my children had ever felt comfortable enough to connect with someone other than their father. Suddenly, that image of the perfect family started popping up again.

He made me feel like I was the only girl on earth. He spoiled me rotten with endless attention. He would serenade me with love songs leaving me cheesing from ear to ear. He was everything I wanted on the list except for one huge problem.

As much as he was operating as a single man, he still had unsolved issues with his baby mother. THEY LIVED TOGETHER! However, I tried to end the situation immediately. I had been there and have a clear story to tell about it. But those roots weren't fully unpacked and this man was too good to be true. He was consistent, and some days, we would talk all night until we both were exhausted. He spent most of his time taking me out. So, he reassured me that they were over and he would start making plans to move out. Time began to fly past and there was no progress being made. I never thought in a million years that I would be the woman in the movies who's asking a man about ending the current relationship status just to have him all to myself.

Soon I started having ongoing and recurring dreams that this man was abusive. He has never laid a hand on me, but there were some red flags as I witnessed his bad temper and how easily he could be angered.

One day after he had gotten into a bad car accident, he called me to pick him up after work. I dropped everything I had going on for the day to come to his aide. As he pulled out the business card to where his car had been towed, I entered the address into my GPS ensuring him that everything was going to be okay. Once we arrived, they gave him the quote to retrieve his car and they took him to the back to look at the damages. I called a few close friends in our circle to see if they could loan him some money to get his car out. Right when the amount was agreed to be loaned, he came out in a panic that his baby mother was on her way and asked me if I could walk back to my car to retrieve his items.

I was in awe. This was the same man that would get mad if I touched my car door or even decided to walk somewhere alone. But all of a sudden his baby mother was magically coming to an address he had to retrieve from a business card and now it was okay for me to do all the things he would yell at me about doing on my own. When I got in the car, I called our friend back to tell him to keep the money since he just threw me away like trash. As I was ending the conversation, he ran to my car apologizing that he was just tripping and came to his senses that she wouldn't even know where he was. I took him where he needed to go, but I knew from that moment forward that something about that relationship was unresolved. Soon there were other women that he began disrespecting me with. His pleading and consistent behaviors started to not matter to me at all. I had to learn that the feeling of love doesn't mean anything without trust, communication, loyalty, and most of all RESPECT.

Another deal breaker was that this man was trying to purposely get me pregnant. One unprotected night of fornication I had with him almost led to impregnation. But after taking the Plan B pill, he started talking about having a baby with me. He started naming unborn children and that was the highlight of the conversation more than him fixing his situation at home. He reassured me it was over and that he was now finding his own place. A few months later, during a weekend retreat for a friend's birthday, he purposely tried to impregnate me. He later confessed that he regrets buying the pill because he wanted me to have his baby.

I believe this was a trap to keep me in his life no matter what he did. I started feeling offended that he wanted to make me another baby mother and not a wife first. They say that before the real one enters your life, sometimes you may run into a counterfeit. This man walked the walk and talked the talk, but at the end of the day, he had no follow through.

I once heard a pastor say that sometimes before you reach the blessing, the devil will set up "gift shops." Gift shops are distractions along the way to rob you of time. Remembering my past, I had to now put my wants and desires aside and tell God to remove anything from my life even if it hurts me. I would rather be hurt now than wait until it gets worse and drain me later.

I had been through too much just to let another man drag me back down to a place of turmoil. Just remembering the pain conflicted with the thought of going down a similar path. I had to let that situation-ship go and acknowledge that I had fallen for him because of comfort.

CROWN OF DOUBLE MINDEDNESS

Double mindedness: wavering in mind; undecided.

Things began to look up for me, but my struggle with sin continued to resurface. I fell into a weird space that led to alcohol abuse and fornication. Being a Christian means that it should be a daily walk and I was so busy looking at what I wanted to be than who I was becoming. I was disappointed in myself that maybe that woman in the frame was far from who I was or who I was becoming.

Just a little key for your spiritual health, I want you to know that the devil uses the same tricks. So, we must be wise not to get caught up.

My Baby Daddy and I began speaking to each other again and one night at my house, we had sex. Tears began to flow down my face and I began asking for forgiveness with every penetration. I pushed him off and told him to stop. A month later, I realized I had missed a period and went to take a test. I was pregnant again. This time I sought out an abortion. I refused to have another baby for this man and was disappointed that I was yet again in the same situation. The devil kept telling me how I wasn't good enough and everywhere I went, people encouraged me to not beat myself up.

I received a prophetic text that stated that whatever God allows is His will and whatever He doesn't allow is also His will. Days later, I went for my examination and the Doctor said that there was no fetal bone structure and that I would have eventually had a miscarriage because there was no baby growing. I went for the surgical abortion and was scared for my life. This time I made a declaration to stop being that 16-year-old girl desperate for attention and comfort. I had to look at where my decisions have gotten me. And I must say that it didn't get me very far. I had to have a made-up mind of who I wanted to be and what I wanted to leave behind as legacy. I couldn't keep going back and forth being on God's team one minute and the devil's playground the next. So, I asked God to walk with me daily and keep me from falling again.

CROWN OF ACCOUNTABILITY

Accountable: require or expected to justify actions or decisions.

Now, I know what you're probably thinking. Poor Girl! She had no support from her father, her mother was tough, and these men mistreated her and now she's a single mother raising two children. That was the thought that I had to be delivered from.

God started shedding light on every situation I had been a victim. Maybe I could have handled certain situations differently with my mom. I was the one that altered my entire world for each man I dealt with. Even when situations were foggy, I stayed put for the continual abuse. I took my crown off to go into valley experiences for temporary satisfaction. My baby father never wanted a relationship with me but I was so focused on changing him and making him commit to our relationship. I always wanted more. I kept going back to him despite the continual red flags. I wanted love and the happy family I envisioned even if it came with pain or anguish. The need for love was the root of the problem. I had to learn how to love myself and to do so, I had to learn how to love my creator because the Bible says that "God is Love". 1 John 4:8.

I also had to tear away my expectations of people. I was hurting myself because I had mentally handed out scripts and casted people for roles that they could never fulfill. I wanted my biological father to give me the attention I deserved. I wanted my mother to be more embracing than critical. I wanted the love, respect, and commitment from each man I dated. Above all, I wanted my stepfather to come back to me. These were expectations that I set out to fulfill on my own without the help of God, which ended in continual heartbreak.

Being heartbroken was the strategy the devil played to keep me bound to alcoholism, complaining, and fornication. These acts of sins robbed me of so many years, even my relationship with God. I was so focused on the empty spaces of my life that I missed many important moments.

We go wrong so many times in our lives by taking matters in our own hands. I had to learn to give my desires, hopes, and dreams over to God and release the control from my hands. Was I wrong for my desire to want love? No! But the way I went about it was wrong. God knows the desires of my heart. But Psalms 37:4 states that to receive the desires of your heart, you must first delight yourself in the Lord.

As new Christians, we seem to get it wrong when we try to heal our own wounds. Healing ourselves is impossible. There are some voids and hurts that only God can heal. The most we could do is have a made-up mind, check our mindset daily, and keep a steady prayer life as well as studying the word of God. If we seek His face, He will surely take care of the rest. I had to make a mental note to stop convincing people who already committed themselves to not value me and kiss them goodbye. Jesus couldn't even convince the world He was the Savior when He walked the earth. But Jesus also knew when to shake the dust and when to go somewhere where He was valued.

Taking accountability in my part of the narrative helped me to forgive. I didn't want to bear the crown of not forgiving along with the other ones I had picked up along the way. I started to look at where I went wrong and how I intentionally laid down to be the walking mat just to feel the comfort of shoes walking over me. The Bible mentioned the kind of woman I was portraying. "They are the kind who worn their way into homes and gain control over gullible women, who are loaded down with sins and are swayed by all kinds of evil desires" (2 Timothy 3:6). I had become the gullible woman and allowed so many men into my space because I was loaded down with resentment and pain that made it easy to choose sin over comfort. But I made the decision never to become that woman anymore. I no longer blamed the men for coming in when I handed them an invitation.

PICK UP YOUR CROWN

I remember asking God to show me who I am in Him. I had picked up all these crowns that weighed me down for so long. He had delivered me through love from each crown. He revealed to me what was in my heart and how I didn't have to carry those crowns much longer. After persistently asking God to reveal who I am in Him, He gave me a reply I had been waiting for.

"Remember that dream I gave you years ago?"

In the dream, I was staring at myself sitting in a big portrait. I was wearing royal purple and gold color attire like an Egyptian princess. And my crown sat nicely upon my head. Everyone was staring at me and I must admit, I was stunning. Then I woke up.

He then said, "Remember that prophet I sent you to tell you to pick up your crown?"

You were in my dream that night. God said, "PICK UP YOUR CROWN" and wear it proudly. You are a daughter of a King.

A crown represents power, victory, and royalty. I was aiming too low in life that I had picked up every crown but my own. God was reassuring me that I belonged to him even while I was trying to belong to everyone else. God says not to put your trust in any man. (Psalms 146:3). I was giving power to men who had let me down instead of staying focused on my Father, the King.

I started to appreciate the chaos because that was God ripping situations and men from my presence. I began to appreciate God for all the corrections and lessons that were taught. "My child, pay attention when the Lord corrects you, and do not be discouraged when He rebukes you. Because the Lord corrects everyone He loves and punishes everyone He accepts as a child. Endure what you suffer as being a father's punishment; Your suffering shows that God is treating you as His child. Was there ever a child who was not punished by his father?" (Hebrews 12:5-7).

I was heartfelt that God saw me as His child. My prayer to God was for Him to teach me how to be a good daughter that I may learn to see Him as my father. Having a relationship with God is much like having any relationship. It requires time, attention, understanding, and despite any outcome, we must choose God no matter the situation.

The purpose of my book is not solely for me to go down memory lane, but to help those who have picked up crowns along the way. Maybe your crown is tainted from past hurts, or a little cracked from past experiences, maybe it's a little dusty because you have walked completely away from your divine calling and who God created you to be. But I am an example that nothing is too hard for God to fix, to find, to mold, and to reveal.

He can show you who you are in Him if you only let Him lead. He can clean you up and give you all your heart's desires. He can answer questions you may have regarding situations you have faced in life. Pain doesn't always last much like a tornado, and rain seems to cease after a while. We can't get so caught up in the pain that we forget the grand picture of who we are created to be.

"When we are punished, it seems to us at the time something to make us sad, not glad. Later, however, those who have been disciplined by such punishment reap the peaceful reward of a righteous life." (Hebrews 12:11)

After all the turmoil, Psalms 139 gives us the blueprint on how to successfully wear the Crown. "Lord you have examined me, and you know me. You know everything I do; from far away you understand all my thoughts. You see me, whether I am working or resting; you know all my actions. Even before I speak, you already know what I will say. You are all around me on every side; you protect me with your power. Your knowledge of me is too deep; it is beyond my understanding. (Psalms 139 1-6). He knew all along the journey I would take and He guided me all through even though I didn't recognize His presence. But it was up to me to change my narrative and stop playing the same record of repetitive behaviors.

I'm a domestic violence survivor, I have my right mind and in great health despite the harm I caused to my body. Both my daughters are healthy and well despite the trauma I faced in pregnancy. I'm not homeless, and all those times I slept in my car or walked home late or was somewhere I was not supposed to be, God protected me in my ignorance. There are so many things I am grateful for and know that I was only saved by God's grace. I want to encourage women and men that there is life beyond the hurt and turmoil they feel. The next part of this book is for your mental, emotional, and spiritual development. It is time to reclaim who you are. Get in your rightful places despite where you are in your walk with God and PICK UP YOUR CROWN!

Past Situations That Are Affecting Me Now

What are some things that are prohibiting you from moving forward? You can write out things that may have affected your growth and harmed you emotionally.

_____

_____

_____

_____

_____

_____

_____

_____

_____

_____

_____

_____

_____

_____

Jessica Simington

Forgiveness

We can't move forward until we forgive others and free ourselves. This was a tough challenge for me, but only God can help you forgive. Is there anyone you have not released and forgiven? Why?

_____

_____

_____

_____

_____

_____

_____

_____

_____

_____

_____

_____

_____

Jessica Simington

Forgiving Yourself

Is there anything that you need to forgive yourself for? What?

_____

_____

_____

_____

_____

_____

_____

_____

_____

_____

_____

_____

_____

_____

_____

Jessica Simington

Questions for God

What are some questions you have for God? Don't be surprised if He starts answering them once you write them down. He already knows what you think or how you feel. Go ahead and write it down just to release it and give it to God to answer.

_____

_____

_____

_____

_____

_____

_____

_____

_____

_____

_____

_____

_____

_____

_____

_____

Jessica Simington

Six-Month Personal Growth Plan

What are some things you wish to accomplish in the next 6 months? You can speak from a mental, emotional, spiritual, or physical standpoint.

Mentally

_____

_____

_____

_____

_____

_____

Emotionally

_____

_____

_____

_____

_____

_____

Jessica Simington

Spiritually

_____

_____

_____

_____

_____

_____

Health

_____

_____

_____

_____

_____

Other

_____

_____

_____

_____

_____

Pick Up Your Crown

Starting today, you are no longer a victim but a King's kid. What declaration would you write yourself to declare changes in your behavior and mindset? This could be set as a reminder to read daily until it's set in stone in your heart. Do not be discouraged if you fall off course. Just simply realign yourself with what you declare over your life, get back up, and move forward. We will not always get it right, but each day is a fresh start.

_____

_____

_____

_____

_____

_____

_____

_____

_____

_____

_____

_____

Jessica Simington

A Letter to God

Write a letter to God. It could be about anything you are thinking. It could be a simple request to show you who you are in Him. It could be a cry for help to move past something or to keep you on the straight path. Whatever you hope to achieve in your walk with God, ask Him in your letter to Him.

_____

_____

_____

_____

_____

_____

_____

_____

_____

_____

_____

_____

_____

_____

Jessica Simington